Flowchart
Science

MOUNTAINS

Richard and Louise Spilsbury

raintree
a Capstone company — publishers for children

Raintree is an imprint of Capstone Global Library Limited, a company incorporated in England and Wales having its registered office at 264 Banbury Road, Oxford, OX2 7DY – Registered company number: 6695582

www.raintree.co.uk
myorders@raintree.co.uk

Produced for Raintree by Calcium Creative Ltd
Printed and bound in India

978 1 3982 0069 2 (hardback)
978 1 3982 0082 1 (paperback)

British Library Cataloguing in Publication Data
A full catalogue record for this book is available from the British Library.

Acknowledgements
We would like to thank the following for permission to reproduce photographs: Picture credits: Cover: Shutterstock: Practicuum (br), Spreadthesign (c); Inside: Shutterstock: A3pfamily: p. 45t; A7880S: p. 24; Alekksall: p. 43; Gudkov AndreyS: p. 37; BGSmith: p. 9t; Neil Burton: p. 31t; Corbac40: p. 6c; Chase Dekker: pp. 18-19; Designua: p. 11; Dennis W Donohue: p. 35; Double Brow Imagery: p. 27r; FJAH: pp. 36-37t; FotoRequest: pp. 22-23; Gherzak: p. 13t; Aldona Griskeviciene: p. 17; Guitar photographer: pp. 40-41; HelloRF Zcool: p. 15t; JerHetrick: p. 23r; Mirek Kijewski: p. 34; Liudmila Kotvitckaia: pp. 1, 26-27; Lillac: p. 5t; Pablo Mazorra: pp. 20-21; Warren Metcalf: p. 19t; Moosehenderson: p. 29b; Moroz Nataliya: pp. 6-7; Nullplus: pp. 44-45; Daniel Prudek: pp. 4-5; Daniel J. Rao: pp. 12-13; Bruce Raynor: p. 41t; SaveJungle: p. 39; Shanvood: p. 33; Smit: pp. 14-15; Joseph Sohm: pp. 8-9; Jan Stria : pp. 30-31; Teri Virbickis: pp. 28-29.

Every effort has been made to contact copyright holders of material reproduced in this book. Any omissions will be rectified in subsequent printings if notice is given to the publisher.

All the internet addresses (URLs) given in this book were valid at the time of going to press. However, due to the dynamic nature of the internet, some addresses may have changed, or sites may have changed or ceased to exist since publication. While the author and publisher regret any inconvenience this may cause readers, no responsibility for any such changes can be accepted by either the author or the publisher.

Contents

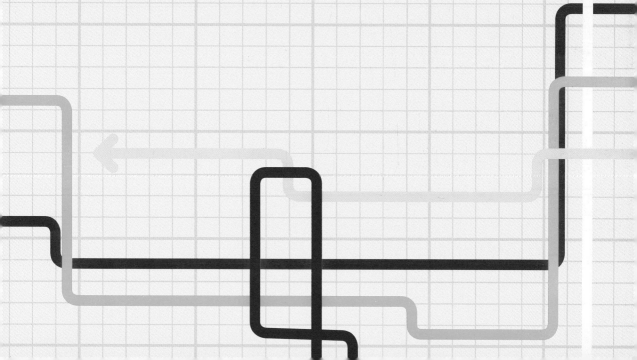

Chapter 1
What are mountains?

A mountain is a large landform that towers high above the surrounding land, often topped by a pointed peak. Mountains are steeper and taller than hills. They provide shelter for a wide variety of amazing plants and animals.

An **ecosystem** is a community made up of living and non-living things **interacting** with one another in an area. Living things include plants and animals and non-living things include the weather, sunlight, water and soil. All ecosystems have their own unique features. The mountain ecosystem includes everything on the mountain, from the cold air and snow at the top, to mountain animals such as goats or gorillas.

Temperatures are very low at the top of many mountains. This mountain is called Ama Dablam, and it is in Nepal.

The non-living features of a mountain ecosystem change depending on the **altitude**. At the bottom of a mountain it might be warm and sunny, but as you climb the mountain it will get colder and be more likely to rain. Higher still, it might be freezing cold with snowfall. The temperature drops by about 1.6° C (3° F) for every 305 metres (1,000 feet) that you go up a mountain. Forests may grow in the warmer soils near the base where the slopes are gentle. Higher up on steep mountainsides, cold winds and rain blast the surface, leaving bare rock and very few plants.

Plants are unable to grow on the craggy peaks of this mountain. The bare rock is exposed and there is very little soil.

Get smart!

At **10,203 m (33,476 ft)** tall, **Mauna Kea** in Hawaii is the highest mountain in the world, but most of this rocky giant is below sea level. Mount Everest is the highest mountain on land. It reaches **8,850 m (29,029 ft)** above sea level.

How mountains form

Mountains form in a variety of ways, and over time, wind, weather and glaciers continue to change them. Dome mountains are found where **magma** below Earth's surface, pushes upwards. It forces the rock above into a rounded bulge. Volcanoes happen when the magma forces its way through the surface and erupts (bursts out). The hot rock is then called **lava**. Volcanic mountains such as these are usually cone-shaped. The lava pours down the side of the erupting volcano and hardens into rock.

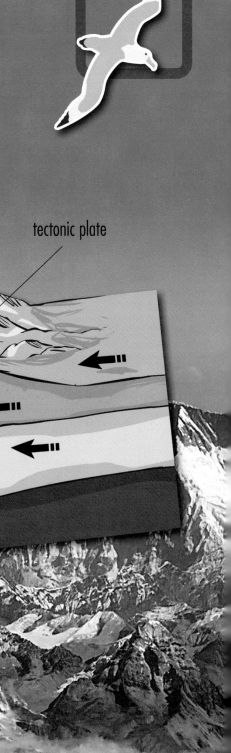

tectonic plate

tectonic plate

As **tectonic plates** beneath Earth's surface meet, one edge can be pushed up to form a mountain.

Fold mountains form when two of the giant tectonic plates that make up Earth's crust (outer layer), collide and push against one another. This causes the land above them to buckle and fold. Huge fold mountain ranges can run through several countries. Block mountains form when faults or cracks in Earth's crust force some materials or blocks of rock straight up and others down.

It is windy and exposed high up on a mountaintop. The wind and rain causes **erosion** of the mountain. Pieces of rock are worn away from the surface and wash or blow away. Erosion can cause cracks in mountain rocks, jagged peaks and other mountain features. Glaciers are huge and incredibly slow-moving rivers of ice that can form in mountains. As they flow downhill, glaciers carry rocks along with them that carve out deep grooves or valleys in mountainsides.

The world's largest mountain ranges are fold mountains. These ranges were formed over millions of years. The Himalayas in Asia are fold mountains.

Get smart!

Some mountains continue to grow. The Himalayas were formed by the collision of two of Earth's tectonic plates. These are still slowly and gradually pushing together and the Himalayas are gradually getting higher.

Mountains of the world

Mountains are found all over the planet. All mountains have different zones from the base to the peaks.

In the Himalayas, the biggest mountain range in the world, the lowest zones have **tropical** plants, including fig and palm trees. The middle zone has plants such as rhododendrons and bamboo. At higher altitudes, above the tree line, it is so cold that nothing grows. The tree line is the region beyond which the conditions are too harsh for trees to grow. The Alps is a huge mountain range in Europe. Its highest mountain is Mont Blanc, which stands 4,807 metres (15,770 feet) tall. High Alpine areas have steep cliffs and fallen rocks with little plant life.

Even in hot countries, tall mountains such as Mount Kenya have snow or ice at the top because their peaks are so high.

Mount Kenya is Africa's second highest mountain at 5,200 m (17,060 ft) tall. On the lowest slopes it is so hot that there are places where there is only grass and scattered trees. Slightly higher, where it is wetter, there are rainforest trees. Higher still, where it is a bit cooler, tall bamboo forests grow. Even higher up, there is open ground with few plants.

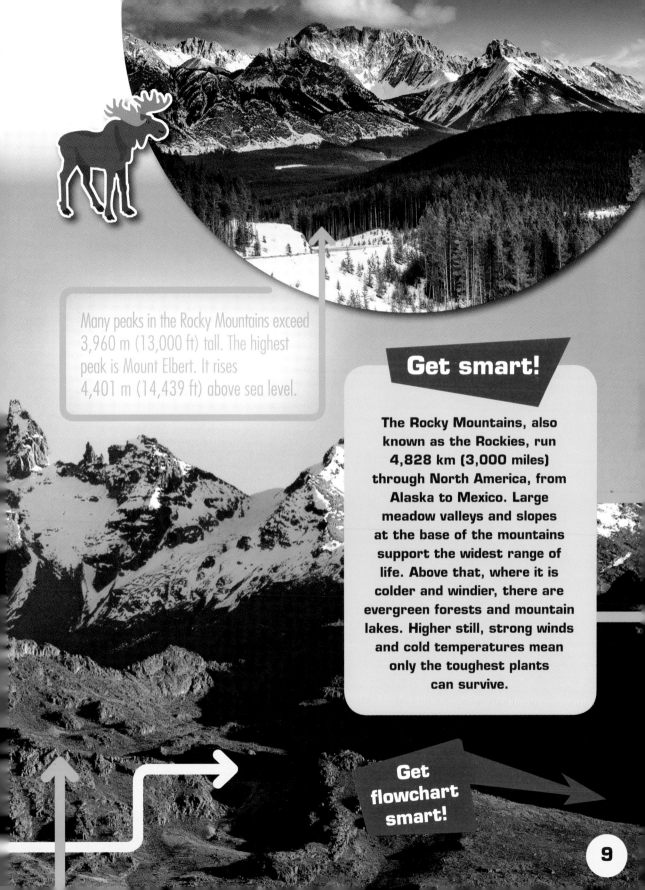

Many peaks in the Rocky Mountains exceed 3,960 m (13,000 ft) tall. The highest peak is Mount Elbert. It rises 4,401 m (14,439 ft) above sea level.

Get smart!

The Rocky Mountains, also known as the Rockies, run 4,828 km (3,000 miles) through North America, from Alaska to Mexico. Large meadow valleys and slopes at the base of the mountains support the widest range of life. Above that, where it is colder and windier, there are evergreen forests and mountain lakes. Higher still, strong winds and cold temperatures mean only the toughest plants can survive.

Get flowchart smart!

How fold mountains form

Let's discover how fold mountains form.

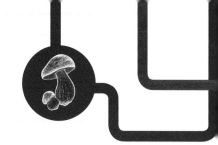

Earth's crust is made up of giant tectonic plates.

This can cause huge mountain ranges that run through several countries.

The Himalayas were formed by the collision of two of Earth's tectonic plates. These are still slowly pushing together and the Himalayas are gradually growing higher.

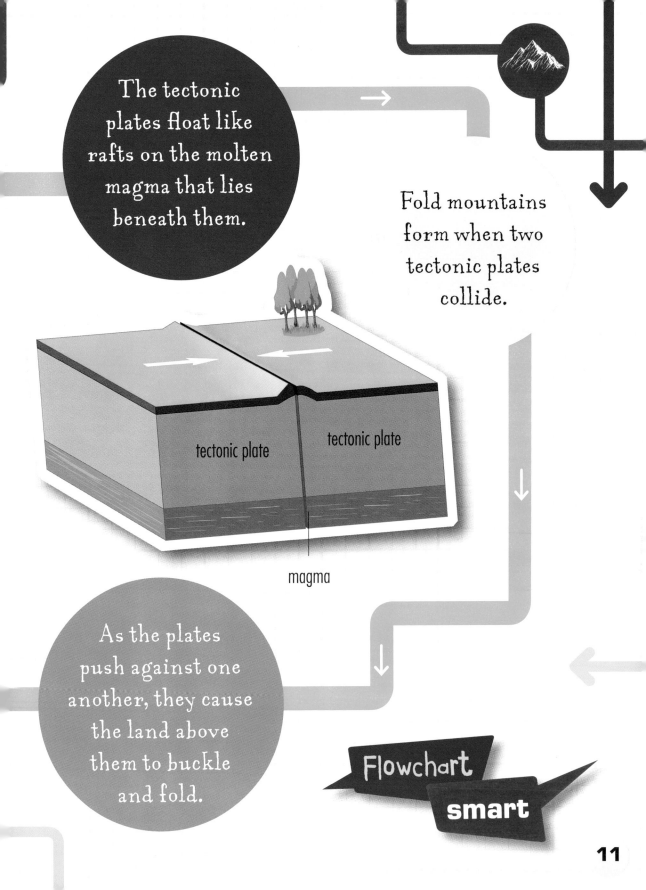

The tectonic plates float like rafts on the molten magma that lies beneath them.

Fold mountains form when two tectonic plates collide.

tectonic plate

tectonic plate

magma

As the plates push against one another, they cause the land above them to buckle and fold.

Flowchart smart

Chapter 2
Mountain plants

Plants have different ways of surviving life in mountain conditions depending on the altitude.

At higher altitudes, many plants are small and grow close to the ground. Above the tree line, the growing season is short because winters are long and harsh. Temperatures are freezing, winds are fierce, and water is often frozen into snow and ice. Plants here are usually small and low growing to keep out of the wind, or they grow in cracks in the rock where it is more sheltered. Plants include tough plants such as heathers and grasses. Lichens are one of just a few living things able to survive on the highest peaks year round. They can even grow on bare rocks.

Other plants have special ways of surviving the cold, too. Moss grows in thick clumps that act like cushions, trapping air and moisture and keeping out the wind. The Arctic gentian grows close to the ground on high mountains in North America and Asia. It forms a thick cluster of fleshy, narrow leaves that hug the ground to seek protection from fierce winds and extreme cold. In spring, the alpine snowbell grows dark-coloured petals. These absorb heat from sunlight, to melt the blanket of snow that helped the plant survive winter, allowing its leaves to reach the light.

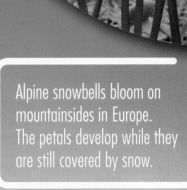

The orange and yellow areas on this area of rock are lichens. They are growing on land above the tree line, which is known as alpine tundra. The word "tundra" means "land of no trees".

Alpine snowbells bloom on mountainsides in Europe. The petals develop while they are still covered by snow.

Get smart!

Lichens are made up of two tiny living things: a fungus and an alga. The alga is a plant-like living thing that can capture sunlight and produce food by photosynthesis. The fungus provides shelter and gathers water. Together, the two form a lichen that can survive harsh weather that would kill a fungus or an alga growing alone.

The tree line

Below the alpine tundra is the tree line. Below the tree line, mountain slopes are often covered in forests.

Higher up the mountains, there is a zone of mostly coniferous trees such as pine. Conifers have thick bark to protect them against the cold. They also grow in a cone shape and have flexible branches to prevent heavy snow building up on them. They keep their leaves all year round so they can capture sunlight and make food by photosynthesis whenever there is sufficient sunlight. They produce their seeds in pine cones, which protect the seeds during the harsh winter. In the lowest zone of some mountain ranges, such as the Alps in Europe, it is warmer and less windy. **Deciduous** trees grow there, such as oak and beech.

These conifers on the Carpathian Mountains in Central and Eastern Europe can survive snowy winters, but only up to the level of the tree line.

Get smart!

Conifers are known as evergreens because they are covered in green leaves all year round. Their needle-like leaves are not as easily damaged by the cold as the broad flat leaves of deciduous trees. This means conifer leaves can begin to photosynthesize quickly, as soon as the temperature exceeds freezing point.

In parts of Asia and Africa, the land approaching the tree line contains conifers and bamboo forests. Bamboo is the largest type of grass in the world. It can grow taller than a lot of trees. The biggest known variety of bamboo can grow to up to 40 m (130 ft) high. The stems have a diameter of 30 cm (1 ft). Bamboo plants can survive in extreme conditions where most other plants cannot. For example, they can live in the Andes and Himalaya mountains at very high altitudes where temperatures can drop far below −20° C (−4° F).

Bamboo grows on mountain slopes that receive plenty of rainfall. This bamboo forest is in the mountains of Kyoto, Japan.

Get flowchart smart!

How lichens survive

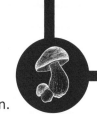

Let's learn how lichens survive at the top of a rocky mountain.

Lichens can grow at the top of a mountain on bare, exposed rock.

The fungus provides shelter and gathers water.

Together, the fungus and the alga form a lichen. It can survive harsh weather that would kill a fungus or an alga growing alone.

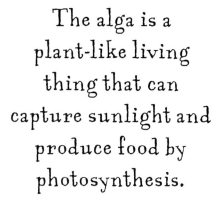

They are made up of two tiny living things: a fungus and an alga.

The alga is a plant-like living thing that can capture sunlight and produce food by photosynthesis.

Flowchart smart

Chapter 3

Animal adaptations

Animals survive in their ecosystems by having special features to help them. These are called **adaptations**.

Some animal adaptations are behavioural, which means that animals have adapted by behaving in a particular way. For example, some mountain animals dig burrows to escape the cold and wind. Others find caves or other sheltered places. Grizzly bears live in the mountains of North America. They find or make large, safe dens to rest in throughout the winter. They stay there until spring, when food becomes abundant again. A den can be a rock cave, tree hollow or a hole in a hillside. Mother bears usually give birth to their cubs while **hibernating** in a den over the winter.

Other adaptations are physical. A grizzly bear and an ibex both have a layer of thick fur to help keep them warm. As well as thick fur, a snow leopard has round, short ears to reduce heat loss. As blood flows through the ears, heat passes from the warm blood into the air: smaller ears mean less heat loss. A snow leopard also has a wide, short nasal cavity that warms the air before it goes into the animal's lungs.

Get smart!

A grizzly bear hibernates in its den over winter. Its heart rate slows down, its temperature drops and it goes to sleep. Doing these things mean that the bear uses a lot less energy. The bear does not feed over winter. It breaks down fat stored in its body from the food it ate during the summer and autumn. Its body uses this fat to make enough energy to survive.

By the time an adult female grizzly bear leaves her den with her new young cubs in the spring, she has lost up to one-third of her body weight.

Snow leopards live at altitudes of 2,990–5,180 m (9,800–17,000 ft). The snow leopard's fur becomes even thicker during the winter. It can also wrap its extra long tail around its body for warmth when needed.

On the move

Mountain slopes can be steep and covered in jagged rocks, with deep cracks and valleys. Areas of ice and snow are also difficult and dangerous to move across. Some animals are well-adapted to mountain travel.

Alpine goats are very agile. They rapidly climb and descend steep and craggy mountain cliffs.

Animals such as the Rocky Mountain goat, bighorn sheep and ibex are among the most sure-footed of all mountain animals. These animals' hooves are adapted to travel over rough rocks at fast speeds and to climb steep cliffs without losing their footing. The hooves are rubbery and flexible, with soft arched undersides to give the animals grip on rocky surfaces.

Birds of **prey** avoid the dangers of steep, rocky mountain terrain by flying over it. Peregrine falcons and eagles soar over the mountainside, looking for food or somewhere to make a nest. Vultures and condors have broad wings that allow them to soar on the winds created by mountains forcing air upwards. Andean condors are huge and have a 3 m (10 ft) wingspan. They spread their wings to glide on air currents above a mountain with very little effort.

Get smart!

The ptarmigan is a bird that lives in the Rocky Mountains. It has feather-covered feet that allow it to walk on top of the snow. The ptarmigan's feathered feet act as snowshoes, spreading its weight over a wider area to preventing the bird from sinking into the snow.

Masters of disguise

Mountain slopes can be very open and exposed, making it hard for prey animals to hide from **predators**. Some mountain animals are adapted to blend in with mountain features to help them stay safe.

Snowshoe hares live in high mountain forests. They change the colour of their fur depending on the season, to help them escape predators. During the winter, their fur is white, which **camouflages** them in the snow. In spring, when the snow melts, the animals' coats change to brown or grey to camouflage them against the rocks and soil. The only part of the hare that does not change colour throughout the year is the tips of its ears, which are always black.

Snowshoe hares have much larger feet and toes than other hares. These adaptations stop them sinking into the snow. Their thick fur keeps them warm.

Get smart!

Pikas are furry mammals that live in western North America. They spend a lot of time searching for food in the mountains. They have brown and black fur that camouflages them as they scurry over the rocks.

Some animals have bright or contrasting colours that make them stand out in their ecosystem, instead of blending in. Warning colours such as these are used by animals that can hurt, sting or poison other animals. The markings warn predators to leave them alone. Monarch butterflies have distinctive bright orange, black and white wings to warn off predators. These butterflies contain toxins (poisonous substances) that they absorb from the milkweed plants they eat as young caterpillars. Birds that do eat monarch butterflies become very sick, which deters them from eating a monarch butterfly again.

Monarchs are beautiful, large butterflies with a wingspan of up to 13 cm (5 in). They taste terrible to the birds that try to eat them.

Get flowchart smart!

How grizzly bears hibernate

Let's take a look at how grizzly bear hibernation works.

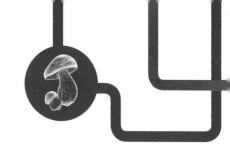

A den can be a rock cave, tree hollow, a hole in a hillside or even among tree roots.

A grizzly bear hibernates in its den over winter.

Inside the den, the bear's heart rate slows, its temperature drops and it goes to sleep. These changes ensure that the bear uses a lot less energy.

The bear does not feed over winter. It breaks down fat stored in its body from the food it ate during summer and autumn. Its body uses this fat to make enough energy to survive until spring.

When a grizzly bear leaves its den in spring, it has lost up to one-third of its body weight.

Flowchart smart

Chapter 4

Food chains

Living things in a mountain ecosystem are linked together through many different food chains, which all begin with plants and trees.

Plants are the first link in mountain food chains because they make their own food. They trap energy from the sun in their leaves and use it to turn **carbon dioxide** gas and water into sugars. This process is called photosynthesis. Plants store the food they make in their body parts, such as in the stems and leaves, to use later. Plant eaters gain this energy when they eat the plants.

Rhododendrons grow on the lower slopes of the Himalayas. They carry out photosynthesis in their green parts. They use the sugars for energy, to grow and produce flowers. Bees feed on nectar in the colourful flowers.

Many insects and other small animals feed on different plant parts. Tiny insects such as glacier fleas and springtails that live high up mountains feed on pieces of plants and **pollen**, which are blown up the mountain from the lower slopes. Mountain pine beetle **larvae** live under the bark of pine trees. They feed on sweet, sticky **sap** from the trunk. Hummingbirds, bees and moths fly in search of mountain flowers from which they can suck up nectar or pollen. The spruce grouse is a bird that eats mostly the needles of pines, spruce and other conifer trees. It also eats the fresh green shoots and leaves of other plants, berries and flowers, as well as some insects, snails and fungi.

Spruce grouse live in evergreen forests in northern and western North America.

Get smart!

Some mountain insects have antifreeze chemicals in their bodies. These keep the water inside their bodies from freezing. This allows them to spend the night frozen to the snow. In the morning, they wait for the sun's heat to warm their dark-coloured bodies and revive them for another day of feeding.

Greedy grazers

Many different animals feed on mountain plants. Some have surprising ways of ensuring they have enough food to survive the cold, harsh winters when plants die back and become buried beneath snow.

Get smart!

Moose are massive animals. Their mouths are strong enough to strip an entire branch of leaves. However, their upper lip is also so flexible and sensitive that it can wrap around and pull a single flower from the ground.

This young moose gorges on willows to build up its fat reserves.

Moose are the biggest deer on the planet yet their diet consists of mainly plants, fruit and seeds. They eat flowering plants and fresh shoots from young trees such as birch or willow. Moose are so tall that it is easier for them to eat taller plants than shorter plants. In winter, they eat shrubs and cones from pine trees. They can also use their large hooves to scrape snow from the ground to expose the moss and lichens beneath, which they eat.

In spring and summer, pikas collect grasses, weeds and wildflowers. They eat some, but lay the majority of the plants they collect out in the sun. The sun dries the plants, which prevents them from going mouldy. Pikas carry mouthfuls of the dried plant foods into their den, where they store them for the winter. They can stay in this den when the weather grows cold and eat the dried grasses they have stored to survive. If they run out, they may leave the den to feed on lichens.

The American pika lives above the tree line in the mountains of northwestern North America. Pikas are active all year and do not hibernate during the winter months.

Predators

Species of predators vary depending on which mountains they live on, though many catch and kill their prey in similar ways.

In the Rocky Mountains, bobcats are fierce predators. The bobcat mainly hunts at night. It sneaks up on its prey quietly. When it is close enough, it takes a giant 3 m (10 ft) leap to land on its prey. A bobcat hunts and eats snowshoe hares, rabbits, mice, birds and squirrels. It usually eats small animals as soon as it kills them. When it catches larger prey, it will eat some and store the rest to eat later.

Lynx, a type of wild cat, lives in the Alps. It hunts animals such as the chamois goat, which in turn feeds on patches of flowers, moss and lichens. Like the bobcat, the lynx sneaks up on its prey and catches it by surprise. It pounces quickly and delivers a deadly bite to the neck. Other alpine predators include birds of prey such as golden eagles. They feed on small animals such as marmots, which come out of their underground burrows to feed on alpine grasses. Golden eagles swoop down on their prey at speeds of more than 240 kilometres (150 miles) per hour, snatching up their victims in their sharp talons.

The lynx has large webbed and furred paws that act like snowshoes.

Get smart!

Sometimes, several different animals eat the same foods. On Mount Kenya, hyraxes, antelopes and colobus monkeys all eat plant foods, and they are all eaten by cats such as servals and leopards. Many food chains linked together are called a food web.

Golden eagles carry prey in their sharp talons to a landing place where they can feed upon it.

Get flowchart smart!

A mountain food chain

Let's follow the links in a mountain food chain.

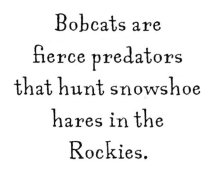

Cranberry plants grow in the Rocky Mountains. They make their own food using energy from the sun in a process called photosynthesis.

Bobcats are fierce predators that hunt snowshoe hares in the Rockies.

Bobcats quietly sneak up on their prey. When close enough, they take a giant leap onto the snowshoe hare. They kill and eat the hare.

Snowshoe hares feed on plant foods such as the mountain cranberries.

Flowchart **smart**

Chapter 5
Mountain interactions

The living and non-living parts of a mountain ecosystem are interconnected. They rely on one another to stay healthy and to survive.

In the Rocky Mountains, the limber pine tree and the Clark's nutcracker have a special relationship. Clark's nutcracker birds pry open the cones on limber pine trees and eat the seeds inside. The birds also bury some of the seeds in different locations so that they can eat them later. The seeds are full of **nutrients** that help the birds survive the harsh winter. The birds bury more seeds than they can eat and forget where they hid some. Those seeds are left to germinate (begin to grow) into new trees in the fresh soil.

Many animals rely on cones and fruit as food. In turn, the trees depend upon these animals to help them disperse (spread) their seeds to different areas where there may be more space to grow. Black bears have a special role in seed dispersal. The seeds from the fruit they eat are excreted in the bears' faeces (waste). The faeces contain nutrients and act as a fertilizer, which improves the chances of the seeds germinating and growing into seedlings.

Many mountain plants rely on bees to transfer pollen from one flower to the next.

Without Clark's Nutcracker feeding on and hiding pine seeds there would be fewer limber pine trees in mountain ecosystems like this one in Yellowstone National Park.

Get smart!

Mountain flowers have brightly coloured petals so insects can find them. When bumblebees, moths and butterflies feed on nectar inside flowers, pollen rubs onto their bodies. They then carry it to new plants. This transfers pollen grains from the male anther of one flower to the female stigma of another. This is called pollination. The plant is then able to make seeds that can grow into new plants.

Helping out

Mountain ecosystems exist in a natural balance. Each part of the ecosystem plays an important role in keeping the whole ecosystem healthy.

Mountain ecosystems have their own waste disposal system. **Scavengers** and **decomposers** break down large quantities of dead animals, plants and other waste. Condors and vultures are scavengers that feed on carrion (dead animals). They break down large animals into smaller pieces that decomposers can use. Decomposers include worms and insects such as maggots and beetles that feed on the remains. They use some of the nutrients they gain from the remains to live, and the rest is released into the soil. Trees and other plants take in these nutrients through their roots and use them to grow.

Mountain gorillas live in high mountain forests in central parts of Africa. They eat a lot of fruit, leaves and bamboo. In doing so, they clear large amounts of plants, which controls plant populations and allows for the renewal and regrowth of certain plant species. Without mountain gorillas eating these plants, the natural balance in the food chain would be disrupted. Bamboo growth would increase, allowing other species who feed on bamboo to also increase. But the extra plant growth would block sunlight and prevent new seeds from thriving. Mountain gorillas also play an important role in seed dispersal.

Get smart!

The condor has no feathers on its head because it usually sticks its head into the carcasses of dead animals to feed. Having a bare head is more hygienic because it keeps flesh and blood from sticking to the bird's feathers.

Griffon vultures are scavengers that feed on carrion, bones and meat. They clear up waste.

Mountain gorillas eat up to about 200 different types of plants and can eat 30 kg (70 lb) of plant foods each day.

Get flowchart smart!

How nutrients are recycled

Follow the steps to see how nutrients are recycled in a mountain ecosystem.

Mountain ecosystems have their own waste disposal system to help them stay healthy.

Decomposers include worms and insects such as maggots and beetles that feed on animal remains. They use some nutrients to live and release the rest into the soil.

Trees and other plants take in these nutrients through their roots and use them to grow.

Scavengers and decomposers break down large quantities of dead animals, plants and other waste.

Condors and vultures are scavengers that feed on carrion. They break down large animals into smaller pieces that decomposers can use.

Flowchart smart

Chapter 6
The future for mountain ecosystems

Many of Earth's mountain ecosystems are under threat because of human activities.

Mountain forests are cut down to clear land for farming and mining, or to sell the wood for timber. This robs plants and animals of their homes and causes other problems. When trees are cut down from mountain slopes, rain and wind are more likely to wash and blow soil and snow down mountainsides, causing avalanches and landslides. Mines, such as coal mines, produce waste that can pollute mountain streams and rivers. Tourists visiting mountains can also cause problems. They may start camp fires that spread and burn forests, they trample mountain plants and they drop litter that can harm animals.

Climate change is another big problem facing mountain ecosystems. As global temperatures increase, insects and other animals that could not formerly survive on mountains because it was too cold there may start to invade them as they grow warmer. This can upset the fragile balance of the ecosystem. For example, in the past, bark beetles that feed on mountain conifer forests died out in cold winters. As winters are becoming warmer, the beetles are multiplying and spreading into new territories. An increase in the number of beetles means more areas of mountain forest are damaged by them.

This fallen pine tree was destroyed by the mountain pine beetle, a type of bark beetle. Mountain pine beetles attack and kill living trees.

Get smart!

Bark beetles lay eggs beneath the bark of pine and fir trees. The larvae that hatch out make feeding tunnels through the living wood in the trees. This damages the tubes that carry water and nutrients around the tree, which eventually kills it.

Fires can get out of control and destroy mountain forests.

Get flowchart smart!

How climate change affects mountains

Discover how climate change is affecting mountain ecosystems.

Climate change is causing average temperatures across the globe to increase.

As global temperatures increase, insects and other animals that could not survive on mountains because it was too cold may start to invade these ecosystems.

An increase in the number of beetles means more areas of mountain forest are being destroyed.

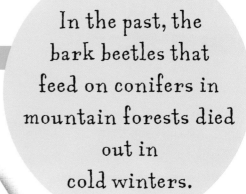

In the past, the bark beetles that feed on conifers in mountain forests died out in cold winters.

As winters grow warmer, the beetles are multiplying and spreading into new territories.

Flowchart smart

Protecting mountain ecosystems

Mountains are important and beautiful ecosystems. People all around the world are working to protect mountains and keep them safe and healthy for the future.

> This scientist is examining the ice in a mountain glacier for signs that it might be melting.

Scientists carry out studies of mountains to help them understand how climate change and **habitat** destruction affect these ecosystems. For example, they study how fast glaciers are melting and what effect this is having on wildlife. Melting glacier water flows into the soil and helps plants grow. If glaciers disappear, this will have an impact on all the wildlife in a mountain ecosystem. By making people and governments aware of these problems, scientists can encourage them to make changes to slow the impacts of climate change.

In some mountain areas, governments have created national parks or reserves. These are areas where people cannot build, mine, clear trees from forests or hunt animals. In other areas, conservation groups are helping people plant trees to replace those that have been cut down in the past. This replenishes mountain ecosystems and protects human communities at the bottom of mountains from landslides and avalanches. Mountains are magnificent ecosystems and we should do all we can to help them have a healthy future.

Planting trees is a very effective way of helping mountain ecosystems.

Get smart!

Giant pandas that live in the mountain forests of central China are one of the rarest animals in the world due to habitat loss. Thanks to conservation efforts, giant panda numbers are slowly increasing. Although giant pandas are still at risk, two-thirds of the population now live safely within a giant panda nature reserve network.

Glossary

adaptations changes to suit a new situation

altitude height above sea level

camouflage blend in with the surroundings

carbon dioxide gas in the air

climate change change in the pattern of the world's weather caused by Earth's atmosphere getting warmer

deciduous tree that loses its leaves in autumn and grows new ones in the spring

decomposers living things that break down waste

ecosystem living and non-living things in a place, interacting with one another

erosion how substances such as rock and soil are worn away and transported by wind or water

evergreen plant that retains its green leaves all year round

food web feeding relationships between food chains in an ecosystem

habitat place where plants and animals live

hibernating going into a type of long sleep to avoid a period of scarce food or bad weather

interacting acting in such a way as to have an effect on one another

larvae young stage of insects and some other animals

lava molten rock once it erupts onto Earth's surface from a volcano

magma hot molten rock below Earth's surface

mammals animals that have hair and produce milk to feed their young

nutrients substances that living things need to survive and grow

photosynthesis process by which green plants make sugary food using the energy in sunlight

pollen grains produced by a flower's male parts

pollination transfer of pollen from the male part of a plant to the female part of a plant so seeds can grow

predators animals that catch and eat other animals

prey animal hunted and eaten by another animal

sap liquid that consists of water and nutrients that circulates inside a plant

scavengers animals that feed on dead animals, plants or waste

tectonic plates giant pieces of rock that fit together like a jigsaw puzzle to form Earth's crust

tropical describes places near the equator, which are warm all year round

Find out more

Books

Animal!: The animal kingdom as you've never seen it before (Knowledge Encyclopedia), DK (DK Children, 2016)

Earth (DK Find out!), DK (DK Children, 2017)

Mountain Food Chains (Food Chains and Webs), Angela Royston (Raintree, 2015)

Mountains (Explorer Travel Guides), Chris Oxlade (Raintree, 2014)

Mountains (Habitat Survival), Melanie Waldron (Raintree, 2012)

Websites

www.bbc.co.uk/bitesize/topics/zvhhvcw/articles/zxg7y4j
Learn more about animal adaptations.

www.bbc.co.uk/bitesize/topics/z849q6f/articles/zvsp92p
Discover more about Earth's biomes.

www.dkfindout.com/uk/animals-and-nature/habitats-and-ecosystems
Find out more about habitats and ecosystems.

Index